Dancing Monkeys In My Soup

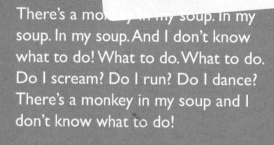

Written by
S.F. Hardy

Illustrated by
Stephanie Hider

There's a monkey in my soup. In my soup. In my soup. And I don't know what to do! What to do. What to do. Do I scream? Do I run? Do I dance? There's a monkey in my soup and I don't know what to do!

There's a monkey in my soup and I don't know what to do! Do I scream? Do I run? Do I dance? There's a monkey in my soup and I don't know what to do!

There's monkeys in my soup. In my soup. In my soup. And I don't know what to do! What to do. What to do. Do I scream? Do I run? Do I dance? There are monkeys in my soup and I don't know what to do!

There's monkeys in my soup. In my soup. In my soup. And I don't know what to do! What to do. What to do. Do I scream? Do I run? Do I dance? There are monkeys in my soup and I don't know what to do!

Dedicated to Syer,
our dancing machine!
-Auntie

Text Copyright: S.F. Hardy
Illustrations Copyright: Stephanie Hider

Editorial Team: A. Cole Books, The Book Doctor and Vicki Hooks Green

All inquiries, comments and updates, submit to, S.F. Hardy at:
sfhardytheauthor@gmail.com or http://sfhardybooks.com.

Shenomenal Ink

Summary: On vacation with his parents, a young boy discovers monkeys dancing in his soup. Everyone scrambles to figure out
what to do to have them removed.

PERU

ISBN: 978-1-7321861-4-9 hardcover
ISBN: 978-1-7321861-5-6 softcover
ISBN 978-1-7321861-6-3 (Spanish)
ISBN 978-1-7321861-7-0 (e-book)
Library of Congress Control Number 2020914904

One day, while on vacation in Peru, I was eating and saw a monkey dancing in my dinner soup! I didn't know what to do, so I went and told my Mom.

"MOM !
HURRY!
COME!

"There's a monkey in my soup!"

"Monkeys don't live in soup.
Only in rainforests, or zoos.
Eat your dinner, Jabbar!

I'm not playing with you!"

I *know* I saw a monkey in my soup,
so I went online to see if I could
find what species of monkey I saw.
I presented my findings to my mother.

"Mom, it's a Pygmy
Marmoset! The world's
smallest monkey is doing
the *Festejo* in my soup.
I can't eat, I won't eat. I
refuse to eat the
soup."

Mom finally decided to come to see for herself.

"See mom, I told you there was a monkey in my soup. There was one, now there's two!"

"Eek!"

Mom screamed. "I'm scared and I don't know what to do. There are two finger-sized monkeys doing the **Marinera** in your soup!" Mom ran outside to get Dad.

"Amid, there are two monkeys in the soup! Come get them out of the house, or I'm not coming back in or speaking to you!"

Dad looked at Mom with a grin. "There aren't any monkeys in the house or in the soup. Monkeys live in rainforests, or zoos, not food."

"Yes! There are, Dad,"

I took his hand. "Let me show you."

When Dad and I got back to the dining room, there were three monkeys doing the **Salsa** in the soup.

"Dad, my research said that the monkeys live in troops, but it didn't say anything about them dancing in soup! I won't be surprised if we close our eyes, and the monkeys multiply."

Sure enough, Dad and I blinked and then there were four monkeys dancing the **Wolosodon** in my soup.

"No way!

his can't be, Son.
don't know what to
o. I've never seen
onkeys outside of the
oo. I've never seen
onkeys dancing in
up!"

"Can you call a zookeeper to get the monkeys out of the soup?"

"Good idea, Jabbar, that's what I'll do!"

"Hello? I need help!

There are monkeys doing the *KuKu* in the soup!
Can you come get them and take them with
 you?" Dad pleaded.

By the time zookeeper arrived, there were exactly
five monkeys dancing. This time, they were doing
the *Zamacueca* in the soup.

The zookeeper tried everything to get the monkeys out of the soup. As a last resort he used chopsticks.

Just when he thought he had them all,
one more monkey appeared.

This one did the splits!
One more monkey made a
total of six.

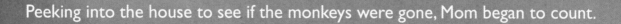

Peeking into the house to see if the monkeys were gone, Mom began to count.

"There are

1,2,3,4,5,6

monkeys dancing
about!"

Mom almost fainted.

When a seventh monkey jumped in, Mom's fright intensified!

She decided to remain hidden outside, but not before monkeys eight and nine came inside. They joined the rest of the monkeys in the soup-dancing fest.

Just when
I thought
no more
monkeys could
fit, and the dancing
would end,
down from
the high ceiling spun
monkey
number

TEN !

There are ten of the world's smallest monkeys dancing in my soup! There seemed to be no getting rid of the dancing monkeys, so I decided to join their dancing monkey troop.

Dear Families and Educators,

Thank you for choosing *Dancing Monkeys in My Soup*! We are
excited for our readers' experiences as our mission is to play a
vital role in empowering children to be extraordinary through
literacy and active exploration. As such, we invite you to go
beyond your reading experience by engaging your youth
with the enclosed family/educator guide. This
supplemental resource will serve to enrich children's
reading experiences, while cultivating a joy for reading.

Enjoy!

S.F. Hardy

Discussion Questions

(To encourage optimal exploration, we decided not to provide an answer key. We did include
resources in which answers can be found. The library is your friend. You may have remote
access to databases with your library card. Happy exploring! :-))

1. What is a pygmy marmoset?

2. What is their natural habitat?

3. Why do you think the monkeys in the book have invaded Jabbar's vacation home?

4. Are pygmy marmosets born in single or multiple births?

5. What is the pygmy marmoset's favorite food?

6. Do the pygmy marmosets have predators?

Why are their colors significant?

Can I have a pygmy marmoset for a pet?

What countries can pygmy marmoset be found? Are these countries landlocked?

). What's a rainforest? What other living things live in the rainforest?

. Did you know, there are different types of rainforest? Can you list them?

2. What languages are spoken in Peru?

3. What does Peru import and export?

4. What's Peru's national song? Try to sing it.

5. What countries do the: Marinera, Festejo, Salsa, Wolosodon, Kuku and Zamacueca
ances originate from? Do the dances have a meaning?

Hands-on Activities

Hold a stick of butter, this is what a pygmy marmoset feels like at its heaviest.

Use an online dictionary to define the word pygmy. Listen to the enunciation.

Let's have fun and be creative! Have students/children make finger pygmy marmoset
uppets.

Have students create their own play using their finger puppets.

Have students create a mock habitat using a shoebox.

Have students create soup or their favorite dish.

Have students explore the differences and benefits between landlocked and coastal.

Have students/children create a petition advocating against the capturing and selling of the pygmy marmoset.

10. Let's dance! Take a field trip or invite a dance instructor to introduce new dance styles.

11. Pygmy marmosets can turn their heads around to see behind their backs. Can you?

12. Character's feelings. Jabbar, was scared and confused when he initially saw the monkey in his soup. Discuss how this changes throughout the story.

13. How many monkey species are there? Take a trip to the library. Divide students up into teams to do a scavenger hunt using books and the internet to determine which team can find the most monkey species. Discuss the difference between old world and new world monkeys.

14. Search YouTube to see the: Marinera, Festejo, Salsa, Wolosodon, Kuku and Zamacueca dances. Can you emulate them?

Resources:

https://animals.sandiegozoo.org/animals/pygmy-marmoset

THE PYGMY MARMOSET Do Your Kids Know This?: A Children's Picture Book . Tanya Turner, 2016.

Facts About the Pygmy Marmoset. Lisa Strattin, 2019.

Dancing Monkeys in My Soup
Word Search

```
C V S X Q O F Z A T X F S F E
P O U E B Y W R R Y T X A L G
R E L F I D E E U S V M T I A
I I Z U B C E K E I I O R Z L
M Y G I M S E R N L T V O A F
A X H V A B O P Y O T H O R U
T U I P I F I V S P M N P B O
E L B T N N A A E U O I R H M
I N E I W C K R B Z K B N R A
A N A Z A G U I A U S R Q I C
K R O T G U M M I V O R E K M
X K I B L D A N C E K G W S D
B O T E S O M R A M Y M G Y P
N N F Z T A T I B A H S G U B
R K S N K K G N T U K L A W N
```

Save The Soup; Find These Words!

AMAZON	HABITAT
BRAZIL	MINI MONKEY
BUGS	PERU
CAMOUFLAGE	PRIMATE
COLUMBIA	PYGMY MARMOSET
DANCE	RAIN FOREST
FAMILY VACATION	SPECIES
FRUIT	TREE SAP
GUMMIVORE	TROOP

Reading is a gift that should be shared with everyone! S.F. Hardy has devoted her personal and professional life to passing the infinite joy of reading to all those she encounters. By day, she lives out one of her wildest dreams as a children's librarian. She is a poet and independent author of: *The Empress' New Hair* and *Like a Salad*. She has been described as a staunch literary advocate with an enormous mission to saturate the children's publishing market with books inclusive of marginalized people, including boys, through her imprint: *Shenomenal Ink*. Hardy, is a native Detroiter and serial graduate of Wayne State University; with majors in Africana Studies, Psychology and Library and Information Science. She loves all things dance—dancing mostly in her head, rarely aloud. She enjoys tasting food from different cultures and exploring the world with family and friends. Hardy spends her spare time, volunteering, designing candles, crocheting and sleeping.

Look for her family reading readiness program: *Get Litty*, where children are empowered to be extraordinary through literacy!

Connect with S.F. Hardy at: sfhardybooks.com or on Facebook at: S.F. Hardy the Author

Illustrator: Stephanie Hider currently lives with her daughter, maltipoo pup in Oklahoma. Random facts: She has an odd but great sense of humor, avid video gamer and sci-fi geek. While she mainly reads nonfiction these days her passion for books has made her a prolific reader. Her favorite word is plethora.

Find out more at: stephisdoodling.com